UNBREAKABLE SPIRIT FROM SHADOWS TO RADIANCE

(From Darkness to Light: A Transformative Journey of Unyielding Hope and Resilience)

Embracing the light within as we rise above the darkest moments

BY
AWTAR KOONAR

Table of Contents

Dedication

This book is dedicated to my parents, whose teachings in hard work, belief, respect, independence, and courage laid the foundation for my unbeatable spirit and equipped me to tackle life's challenges.

To my spouse and friends, whose unwavering support helped me navigate the darkest times after my accident in 2000. To my son, my closest friend, whose memory continues to inspire me four years after his passing in 2020, he was truly proud of how I managed the ongoing challenges stemming from that accident.

In deepest gratitude to Sai Baba ji, whose divine blessings became my beacon of hope during life's most challenging moments. As he proclaimed, "Where there is Faith, there is Love; Where there is Love, there is Truth; Where there is Truth, there is Peace; Where there is Peace, there is Bliss; And where there is Bliss, there is God!" Through unwavering faith, I learned that no challenge is insurmountable when divine guidance illuminates the path.

To all who find themselves in the shadows, may this journey of faith, blessings, meditation, and resilience light your way to radiance. For everyone striving to overcome adversity and find strength within themselves, may this book serve as a beacon of hope and a testament to the power of the human spirit—guided by faith, sustained by gratitude and willpower, and transformed by resilience.

Preface

This book is a profound journey through the intricate landscape of human resilience, tracing a path from the vibrant villages of Punjab, India, to the complex corridors of Canadian life. It is more than a memoir; it is a blueprint for survival, transformation, and spiritual awakening.

At its core, this narrative confronts life's most challenging moments: mistaken identity, a devastating accident that threatened to derail everything, serious legal charges of dangerous driving causing death, and the heart-wrenching loss of a child. Yet, these are not stories of defeat but rather testaments to the extraordinary power of faith, divine grace, and the unwavering human spirit.

Through deep personal experiences, I reveal how spiritual anchors can transform seemingly insurmountable challenges. This book explores the hidden powers within the human mind and how, when harnessed positively, these can change your life forever. It demonstrates how faith, positive attitude, determination, and courage provide enormous opportunities for self-realization, inner harmony, and healing.

The journey described here is not about theories or history but about real-life experiences, values, and the profound impact of one's upbringing. It delves into the astonishing power of prayers and meditation, showing how true faith can bring inner peace and even lead to transformative spiritual visions.

As you journey through these chapters, you will discover that while major life events may be predestined, how we navigate between these is shaped by our actions, karma, and attitude. You'll learn about the crucial role of hope in life's journey and how faith, prayers, self-esteem, and determination can influence our fate and destiny.

This book is a raw and honest exploration of survival that transcends mere storytelling. It offers practical insights into harnessing faith during crises, transforming grief into strength, and maintaining hope when circumstances seem hopeless. It also delves into the profound connection between spiritual beliefs and personal resilience, highlighting how our greatest challenges often become our most powerful teachers.

Your internal belief, faith, and willpower are powerful healers, capable of transforming even your physical health. This book aims to inspire readers by showing how an ordinary person can achieve his dreams through a positive attitude, faith, willpower, determination, and learning from mistakes. The sky truly is the limit when we harness these inner resources.

As you embark on this journey with me, prepare to be challenged, inspired, and transformed. May this narrative serve as a beacon of hope, guiding you toward your own path of resilience and spiritual growth.

Awtar koonar

.

Author's Note

The events described in this book are drawn from a tapestry of sources, woven together to create a comprehensive narrative of my journey. While my personal experiences and memories form the foundation, this account has been enriched by the perspectives of family, friends, and medical professionals who were integral to my story.

A significant portion of the narrative, particularly the sections detailing my near-death experience and recovery, has been meticulously reconstructed from a diary I maintained during that challenging period. This contemporaneous record has proven invaluable in capturing raw emotions and vivid details that might otherwise have faded with time.

In addition to these personal sources, I've incorporated information from official records and testimonies. The accounts of the accident and subsequent legal proceedings include inputs provided by police reports and my lawyer, ensuring a balanced and accurate representation of these critical events.

While human memory can be fallible, I have made every effort to recount these events as accurately and truthfully as possible. Where recollections diverged or details were unclear, I sought to present the most consistent and plausible account based on all available information.

As you read this account, I invite you to reflect on your own journey and the untapped reservoirs of strength within you. May this story serve as a testament to the resilience of the human spirit and the power of faith, meditation, determination, and positive thinking in overcoming life's greatest challenges.

Chapter 1: The Fateful Journey

Fatal accident in heavy fog

CBC News · Posted: Jul 28, 2000 1:38 AM EDT | Last Updated: July 28, 2000

A 29-year-old Renfrew man has bee killed in an early morning collision on Highway 17 near Renfrew.

Bryce Leskie was driving in heavy fog just before six a.m. on Friday morning when he collided with a car driven by 50-year-old Awtar Koonar of Kanata.

Police say Koonar is in the Ottawa Hospital with life threatening injuries.

In 1999, a pivotal moment altered the course of my family's life. My son, Ranjeet, after four dedicated years at Lakehead University, received an unexpected letter stating he needed to retake one course to graduate from the University. This shocking news meant a fifth year of study, 1500 kilometers from home. Every September, my wife and I drove him to Lakehead University in Thunder Bay, and every May, we drove him home. This time, I offered to drive him a few weeks before classes resumed to help him find and set up an apartment.

The morning of July 28, 2000, dawned bright with promise. As we prepared to leave for Thunder Bay, my wife admired our gleaming white Cadillac. With a wave of goodbye, my son and I set off westward, the air filled with anticipation and easy conversation.

About 50 kilometers into our trip, we encountered a dense fog that engulfed us like a thick, white blanket. Visibility plummeted until we could barely see a few feet ahead. We cautiously followed the taillights of a gas tanker, trusting the truck driver's expertise in these treacherous conditions.

As I contemplated pulling over at the next town to wait for the fog to clear, the tanker suddenly veered right. In that moment of confusion, I noticed a dim light approaching head-on. Realizing the imminent danger, I instinctively swerved towards the left ditch. Tragically, the oncoming vehicle made the same decision, leading to a catastrophic head-on collision.

The impact was violent and sudden. Our Cadillac took the brunt of the hit on the driver's side as I tried to save my son. Pain and disorientation overwhelmed me as I lost all sensation in my legs and feet. My son, though shaken and bruised from his seatbelt, was miraculously unharmed.

In the chaotic aftermath of the crash, I have fragmented memories of Canadian military personnel arriving first on the scene, followed quickly by police, ambulance, and firefighters. The fire crew worked tirelessly to free me from the mangled wreckage, but I was trapped by the severe damage to the driver's side door. As my consciousness faded in and out, I felt utterly helpless, unaware that this moment would mark the beginning of a profound journey that would change my understanding of life itself.

Between Life and Death: Embracing the Cosmic Connection

As consciousness slipped away in the wreckage of the car, I found myself in a liminal state where the boundaries between life and death blurred. The acrid smell of smoke and twisted metal faded, replaced by an otherworldly peace. In the years that followed, vivid memories of this experience surfaced, illuminating a profound journey beyond the physical realm.

In the immediate aftermath of the accident, as I lay in critical condition, my consciousness seemed to shift. My first awareness was of finding myself in a breathtakingly beautiful garden. The flowers were enormous, vibrant, and incredibly colorful - reminiscent of giant sunflowers or dahlias. I was surrounded by these, enveloped in their beauty and serenity. In this place, time held no meaning, and I felt a profound sense of belonging as if returning to a familiar place. While I didn't see or hear anyone else, I wasn't alone. There was an all-encompassing presence, a feeling of being connected to something greater than myself.

As this experience unfolded, I was enveloped by an undeniable divine presence that radiated waves of perfect peace, contentment, and unconditional love. In this serene state, I experienced what I can only describe as a life review. Communication transcended spoken words. The divine messenger conveyed, "So, you are going back." I affirmed silently, "Yes." When asked, "Why?" my answer came from deep within: "Because my mother and my children need me." In that moment of clarity, I began to descend through a dark tunnel. The light faded until I found myself in the hospital's Intensive Care Unit, surrounded by medical staff and my family. The stark realization hit me: I could not see or feel my feet.

This near-death experience profoundly shaped my understanding of life and our connection to something greater. It reminded me that even in our darkest moments, we are surrounded by an omnipresent love. The accident not only changed my life but also deeply impacted my family and friends. My son, who walked away with minor bruises, bore emotional scars from witnessing such trauma. My mother's face was etched with pain and worry during her visits, her strength barely concealing her fear for my future.

My recovery journey would be long and challenging, facing serious medical conditions related to my body, crushed feet, and heart. The uncertainty of whether I would ever walk again or be confined to a wheelchair weighed heavily on me, affecting me emotionally and mentally.

Through this experience, I gained new insights into my own strength and faith, as well as the profound connections we share with the universe and our loved ones. My beliefs shifted, recognizing a deep spiritual dimension to life. Each day became a lesson in patience, gratitude, and the power of human resilience.

This encounter with the beyond left an indelible mark on my soul, profoundly influencing my perspective on life, death, and the nature of existence. It became a source of comfort and strength in the challenging times that followed, a reminder of the peace that exists beyond our physical reality.

Chapter 2: Between Two Worlds - ICU

After the accident, I found myself in the Intensive Care Unit (ICU) at Civic Hospital in Ottawa, suspended between life and uncertainty. The severity of my injuries was immediately apparent, with both feet elevated and intense pain coursing through my body like electric currents. The medical staff administered potent painkillers and critical medications, creating a pharmaceutical shield against the trauma. Doctors conducted numerous tests, investigating potential neck injuries, chest trauma, and complex damage to my groin area, feet, and legs. The pain concentrated in my feet was the most excruciating, a constant reminder of the accident's impact.

My world had shrunk to the sterile confines of the ICU. Visitors were strictly limited to my wife, while friends were turned away, adhering to critical care protocols. My body was so dramatically swollen that I was barely recognizable, a testament to the accident's brutal force.

The combination of injuries, trauma, and medications kept me in a twilight state of semi-consciousness. I drifted between fragmented awareness and deep medicinal sleep, with my body's survival mechanism working over time.

Throughout the challenging five-day ICU stay, the staff's exceptional care was crucial. Their unwavering professionalism was instrumental in managing my critical condition, laying the groundwork for my eventual transfer to the hospital's general ward.

An unexpected incident occurred when, in a rare moment of semi-consciousness, I requested chicken curry with naan from my wife. Despite momentarily enjoying the meal, my unprepared system reacted violently, causing extreme pain. This became a poignant lesson in the holistic nature of recovery, emphasizing the importance of patience and careful navigation.

Flashback - Resilience and Reflection: "Drawing Strength from Childhood Memories"

In the hazy realm between consciousness and dreams, I find myself drifting through vivid memories of my childhood in Punjab. These are not mere recollections but powerful visions that seem to envelop me, offering solace and strength as I lay in the ICU.

The dream unfolds in my small village in Punjab, where the scent of rain-soaked earth fills the air, and nature's joyful sounds surround me. Memories of my childhood flood back, of a time when my father wore two important hats in our community. He was both the respected headmaster of our village school and the person in charge of the local post office. As the scene crystallizes, my father appears before me, his eyes gleaming with pride. "My son," his voice echoes in my mind, "do you remember when I would entrust you with managing the post office during my short absences?" He continues, his voice warm with approval, "That task showed your true potential and perseverance. You never gave up, even when faced with challenges." My mother's presence brings a wave of warmth. Her whispered words resonate in my spirit: "You've always had a special light within you. Let it guide you through the darkest times." In this dream state, I feel her unwavering support as if it were a tangible force.

The scene shifts to our nightly gatherings around the coal fireplace. Family and friends share the day's events, village gossip flows freely, and we playfully tease our elder brother about admiring glances from girls. Even in my unconscious state, I can feel the strength of those family bonds and the importance of laughter in the face of adversity.

Flashes of other memories surface - managing the village post office as a young boy, my father's pride in his sons becoming engineers, and the joy of community service. Each vision reinforces values of perseverance, hard work, and giving back to others.

As I gradually regain consciousness, my dream memories crystallize into a profound and powerful realization. The beeping of hospital machines fades in, but my inner voice rises above these: "I am the product of love, trust, and perseverance. I've overcome challenges before. I can do anything. I will heal. I will recover. I will thrive."

Slowly, I open my eyes to the reality of the ICU. However, I feel fortified by the lessons from my dream - confidence in my abilities, the importance of hard work and perseverance, the strength found in family and community bonds, and the fulfillment that comes from serving others. These values, ingrained in me since childhood, now serve as a wellspring of strength as I face this new challenge.

With each breath, I remind myself that I carry within me the resilience, faith, and determination nurtured by my upbringing. These qualities will guide me through this ordeal and beyond, just as these have throughout my life. The dream may have faded, but its impact remains, infusing me with the courage and hope needed for the journey ahead.

After five days in the Intensive Care Unit (ICU), the surgeons determined that my condition had stabilized sufficiently to allow for a transfer to a regular hospital ward. This decision marked a significant milestone in my long recovery journey. While I was no longer in critical condition, I still required continuous medical care and monitoring.

In the regular ward, the level of care would be different from the intensive, one-on-one attention provided in the ICU. I would need to adapt to a new environment with less frequent monitoring and potentially more independence in basic activities. This transition, while positive, could also bring anxiety as I adjusted to reduced medical supervision.

Chapter 3: Stepping Back From The Brink: Hospital Ward

My transition from the Intensive Care Unit (ICU) to the general ward marked a pivotal moment in my recovery journey. This period was a crucible of physical challenges, emotional complexity, and profound uncertainty. Each moment balanced precariously between survival and healing, medical intervention and human resilience, all underpinned by an unwavering faith in the Creator.

After five days in the ICU, I was transferred to a single room in the general ward at the Civic Hospital. This move, while signifying progress, brought its own set of challenges. The shift from constant monitoring to a less intensive care environment can be daunting for patients and families alike. Despite the change, I remained under strong pain medications and required constant care. The hospital staff, whom I saw as blessings in disguise, assisted me with daily tasks like sponge baths and meals, reflecting the complex nature of my recovery.

Family Support and Visitors

My mother, in her late 70s, embarked on a journey from Calgary to be by my side during my most vulnerable moment. Her arrival was more than a physical presence; it was a profound manifestation of unconditional maternal love. Despite her advanced age, she demonstrated remarkable strength and resilience, traveling across provinces to support her critically injured son.

Her eyes told a complex story of love, fear, and hope. Each glance was laden with unspoken emotions, a mixture of deep maternal concern and unwavering faith in my recovery. Her silent vigil at my bedside felt like a sacred ritual, a spiritual connection that transcended medical prognosis. Her presence was a divine blessing, radiating healing energy and reinforcing my own belief in the power of recovery.

My wife's regular hospital visits were equally crucial to my healing journey. She balanced emotional support with practical care, ensuring I was supported during this challenging period.

Beyond immediate family, friends and colleagues who learned about the accident also came to visit. These visits were more than social courtesies; these were lifelines of emotional support. Each visitor brought a unique energy—some offering words of encouragement, others providing silent companionship.

This experience profoundly underscored the critical role of social support in medical recovery. The emotional nourishment provided by family and friends contributed significantly to my healing process, demonstrating that recovery is not just a physical journey but a holistic experience involving mental, emotional, and spiritual dimensions.

The collective love, prayers, and support I received during this period became a powerful catalyst in my recovery, reinforcing my belief in the extraordinary healing power of human connection.

Legal Concerns, Media Attention, and Police Visit

Four days after my transfer to the hospital ward, while still heavily medicated and drifting in and out of consciousness, I received an unexpected visit from a police officer and a detective. Despite my compromised state, I endeavored to provide them with what information I could recall about the accident. I later learned that they had also interviewed my son, who was still in a state of shock from the accident. The realization that this process hadn't fully considered his emotional vulnerability troubled me deeply.

Recognizing the potential legal ramifications of the situation, my father-in-law urged my wife to secure legal representation. Heeding his advice, she reached out to Cary Mclelland, a highly selective lawyer known for his discerning approach to case selection. This proactive step would prove crucial in navigating the complex legal landscape that lay ahead.

Meanwhile, the outside world was abuzz with news of my accident, which had been reported across various media platforms. A nurse, to keep me informed, shared that she had heard about the accident on TV. However, her well-intentioned update came with shocking news: the other driver hadn't survived the collision.

This revelation was quickly followed by another devastating piece of information - I was being charged with dangerous driving, causing death. The weight of this news was overwhelming, sending my mind into a tailspin. As I lay there, still grappling with my own physical recovery, I was now faced with the crushing reality of a life lost and the looming specter of serious legal consequences.

The convergence of my precarious health, the tragic outcome for the other driver, and the potential legal repercussions created a perfect storm of anxiety and uncertainty. As I struggled to process this information, my concerns about an uncertain future intensified, compounded by the profound sadness for the loss of life. This moment marked the beginning of a complex journey that would challenge me not just physically but emotionally, ethically, and legally as well.

Emotional and Spiritual Struggles

The combination of constant pain, anxiety, and worries about an unknown future led to many sleepless nights. There were moments when I felt everything was going wrong, unsure how long I could keep my head above water. However, my strong faith became a pillar of support, an unbreakable connection to the Creator. I would pray and practice relaxation techniques, leaving my worries in the hands of a higher power.

This period in the hospital ward was a crucial step in my journey from the shadows of near death to the radiance of recovery. It tested my physical endurance, emotional resilience, and spiritual strength. Yet, with each passing day, I felt the Creator's presence, guiding me toward healing and renewal. My faith, coupled with the support of my loved ones and the dedicated medical staff, became the foundation upon which I would rebuild my life, one blessed moment at a time.

For those facing similar struggles, remember that even in the darkest moments, faith and the support of loved ones can provide immeasurable strength. Embrace the help offered by medical professionals, lean on your support system, and never underestimate the power of your inner resilience. Your journey, though challenging, can lead to profound personal growth and a deeper appreciation for life's blessings.

A Journey of Recovery: Challenges and Blessings

Family Dynamics and Emotional Landscape

My recovery journey was a complex tapestry woven with both challenges and blessings. While I faced significant physical hurdles, the emotional landscape was equally intricate, revealing painful family dynamics. The manner in which my in-laws treated my mother was distressing, yet I concealed my feelings to protect her from additional worry. This highlights how traumatic conditions and hospitalization can affect not only the patient but also their family members.

Medical Challenges and Continuity of Care

After being transferred to the general ward from the ICU, I encountered another challenge when my main surgeon went on vacation, leaving his trainee in charge of my care. The removal of numerous stitches, particularly in my left foot, was an agonizing experience. Fortunately, a nurse with armed forces experience proved to be a godsend, using a special device to streamline the stitch removal process. His expertise exemplified how healthcare providers with diverse backgrounds can contribute unique skills to patient care.

Comprehensive Medical Assessment

During my extended stay at the hospital, I underwent a series of tests to assess potential injuries to my heart, lungs, chest, and neck. ECG tests revealed that I had suffered a minor heart attack, which I chose to conceal from my family and friends to spare them additional worry. As a precautionary measure, I wore a cervical collar to protect my cervical spine and provide stability.

Every day, Dr. Charles, my surgeon's trainee, would visit to check on my progress. My left foot had sustained severe damage, with the possibility of amputation looming over me. The wounds on both feet were extensive and carried a high risk of infection. Dr. Charles's daily treatments were necessary but excruciatingly painful.

Transition to Rehabilitation

After 21 days in the hospital, Dr. O'Neil, my orthopedic surgeon, cleared me to transfer to a convalescent facility. This transition marked a significant milestone in my recovery journey—moving from acute care to a rehabilitation setting. The discharge planning process was comprehensive and aligned with best practices in care coordination.

TD Insurance (formerly Monnex Insurance) demonstrated exceptional support during this time. Their representative, Vicki, took charge of all details regarding my transfer, exemplifying a coordinated transition approach recommended in quality care standards. They arranged for a beautiful room in a senior's residence on Montreal Road and coordinated all transportation needs.

A New Phase of Recovery

In August 2000, I was transferred to the senior's home, marking the beginning of a new phase in my recovery. The smooth execution of this transfer highlighted the importance of coordinated efforts between healthcare providers, social services, and insurance companies in ensuring successful transitions for patients with complex needs.

Throughout this challenging period, the unwavering support from hospital staff, family, and TD Insurance was crucial to my recovery. My strong spiritual foundation, instilled by my parents and reinforced by my elder brother's support, provided me with the strength to navigate this difficult time. This experience demonstrated the positive impact that comprehensive support can have on a patient's recovery journey as I moved forward into rehabilitation with renewed hope and strength.

Chapter 4: Canadian Crossroads: A Journey of Transformation

As I lay in my hospital bed, memories of my journey from Punjab to Canada flooded my mind, revealing a tapestry of divine interventions that shaped my path. My thoughts drifted to my university days in Punjab when my oldest brother, who settled in Alberta after his Master's degree, sponsored my immigration, setting in motion a plan greater than I could have imagined.

In 1970, during my third year of studies, I received a permanent visa to Canada. However, prioritizing my education, I chose to defer. The Canadian high commissioner, recognizing my commitment, suggested my brother reapply in a year. This seemingly routine bureaucratic process now appeared as a carefully orchestrated series of events guiding me toward my destiny.

The ease with which I obtained a visa the second time upon my brother's reapplication spoke volumes about the unseen forces at work. Each step, from the initial sponsorship to the Canadian high commissioner's understanding, formed a crucial piece in the mosaic of my life's journey. This reflection filled me with profound gratitude for the subtle yet powerful ways divine intervention had guided me from the familiar comforts of Punjab to the vast opportunities awaiting me in Canada.

Embracing New Opportunities: My Journey to The University of Ottawa

My Canadian journey began with my brother's warm welcome in Edmonton before Calgary became my home for the next year. This period was marked by both challenges and growth, particularly as I faced discrimination during my job search in Calgary. Despite these setbacks, I remained resolute, drawing strength from my parents' blessings, my brother's encouragement, and unwavering faith.

While working odd jobs to support myself, I simultaneously applied to Canadian universities for a master's program in engineering. I received acceptance from eight universities across Canada. After careful consideration of the programs and financial support offered, I chose the University of Ottawa.

In September 1971, I embarked on a new chapter, taking a train from Calgary to Ottawa to begin my studies. This journey symbolized not just a physical transition but the start of a transformative educational experience in Canada's capital.

Ottawa: A New Chapter

My university days in Ottawa were truly blessed, filled with laughter, friendships, and personal growth. As an international student, I initially faced challenges adjusting to the new academic system, but the welcoming community at uOttawa made the transition smoother. The multicultural environment allowed me to share my culture while learning from others, fostering a sense of global citizenship.

A significant highlight of my time at uOttawa was becoming president of the Indian Students Association, which had over 200 members. This role revealed my leadership potential and provided a platform to connect with fellow Indian students, the broader community, and alumni. Our association organized cultural events, celebrated festivals, and showed Indian movies, creating a home away from home for the Indian diaspora. These experiences enriched my university life beyond academics and taught me the value of collaboration and cultural exchange.

My first day at the University remains vivid in my memory, especially my meeting with Dr. Louis Birta, Chairperson of the Computer Sciences faculty, my advisor. He asked if I knew computers and especially Fortran programming language. When I admitted to having no prior knowledge of computers or Fortran, a computer language essential for my studies, his skepticism was evident. He questioned whether he had admitted the right candidate but gave me three weeks to learn the Fortran language. With no alternative, I embraced the challenge wholeheartedly. Despite his recommendation to take only three courses at the Master's level, I registered for five, fully aware that failing two would mean expulsion from the University.

Balancing coursework with learning Fortran in the evenings at the computer center was daunting, especially while maintaining my social commitments. However, with determination and divine support, I not only mastered the language within the given timeframe but also began teaching it to undergraduate students within a month. This experience significantly improved my proficiency and became invaluable for my thesis work. Passing all five courses with excellent grades was a testament to faith and hard work.

Dr. Birta's initial doubts eventually turned into confidence in my abilities. His guidance and support throughout my thesis work were remarkable and truly a blessing. Reflecting on these memories from my hospital bed brought me a renewed sense of strength. The same universe that guided me through those early challenges in Canada was surely with me now, helping me navigate this new obstacle of recovery.

A Divine Intervention: The CAE Connection

As I lay in the hospital bed, reflecting on my journey, I realized how a series of seemingly chance encounters had shaped my professional life. It all began with my good friend N. Murti, a true godsend, who encouraged me to apply for a position at CAE, where he worked. His selfless act of kindness, expecting nothing in return, exemplified the kind of person I aspired to be. Through his recommendation, I secured my first job as a software engineer, marking the beginning of a transformative professional journey. This experience taught me the power of networking and the impact one person can have on another's life trajectory.

Mentors and Guiding Lights

At CAE, I was blessed to encounter two remarkable individuals who further shaped my path. My supervisor, Mr. Raj Shaw, offered invaluable support and mentorship, nurturing my professional growth. My manager, Mr. Stuart McDonald—a Scottish gentleman—was a character of intelligence and discernment who recognized and appreciated dedication and hard work. Their presence in my life felt like a reward for good karma from previous lives, a reminder of the interconnectedness of our actions across time. These relationships taught me the importance of mentorship and the lasting impact of positive leadership.

Professional Growth and Challenges

The confidence instilled in me by my parents blossomed at CAE Electronics, an exemplary company that truly valued its employees. This experience provided numerous lessons that would shape my future career, teaching me the importance of a supportive work environment. Eventually, I found myself at Environment Canada, where I faced new challenges as one of the few people of color in my workplace. Through blessings, hard work, persistence, and a deep respect for my management and colleagues, I flourished. I gained the respect of my managers and had the privilege of working on multi-million-dollar projects, learning to navigate and succeed in diverse professional environments.

It was during my time at Environment Canada that my life-altering accident occurred, setting me on an unexpected path of recovery and self-discovery. As I lay in the hospital bed, I couldn't help but marvel at the journey that had led me to this point and the profound impact that mentorship and professional relationships had on shaping my career and personal growth.

Chapter 5: Convalescent Care:
A Journey of Recovery and Resilience

The Senior's Home: A Crucible of Recovery and Resilience

My journey at the senior's home on Montreal Road began after a 17-day stay in the hospital ward following my time in the Intensive Care Unit (ICU). The facility provided a studio apartment with essential amenities, creating a nurturing environment for my healing process. As I initially required 24/7 support, being unable to walk or use a wheelchair independently, the staff, along with my insurance company, provided comprehensive care that extended beyond basic medical needs, offering crucial support during this challenging time.

Regular Visits to The Hospital

During my stay at the senior's home, I made regular visits to the hospital for medical check-ups and to have the plasters on both my feet changed. It was during one of these visits that I finally asked the medical staff about the events immediately following my accident. They explained that due to the severity of my injuries, I had been airlifted from Highway 17 in Renfrew County to the Civic Hospital, where I was immediately admitted to the ICU. The medical team recounted how, upon my arrival at the hospital, Dr. O'Neil and his team performed an emergency seven-hour surgery to save my feet. They revealed that at one point, the amputation of my left foot was considered, but my wife had refused to give consent.

The Journey to Recovery

As my recovery progressed at the senior's home, I gradually gained more independence. After two weeks, I was provided with a wheelchair along with intensive training, granting me some autonomy in daily activities. This training was crucial in helping me regain my mobility and confidence.

A VON nurse visited twice daily to tend to my wounds and administer blood thinner injections in my stomach, a painful but necessary process to prevent complications. The facility took care of meals, offering crucial relief during this challenging time.

Regular visits from colleagues, friends, and family became my lifeline, with coworkers from the Ice and Marine Services of Environment Canada visiting every Friday. These social interactions were vital for my emotional well-being and recovery.

A particularly memorable moment was my birthday celebration in the party hall at my senior's home, arranged by my wife, where she invited all our friends and a few colleagues. This event was full of fun, with some friends entertaining through songs. It significantly boosted my morale and made me feel valued, providing a much-needed emotional uplift.

Return To Work

About 60 days into my stay at the senior home, I expressed a desire to return to work, surprising both my employer and the insurance company. My insurance company was initially concerned but eventually agreed and provided transportation to and from my work at the senior home. My employer showed exceptional support by modifying the workspace to accommodate my wheelchair needs. This marked the beginning of my journey back to normalcy and played a crucial role in my psychological recovery.

Medical Milestones and Challenges

My medical journey was marked by significant milestones and challenges. The hospital visits for plaster changes revealed the extent of my injuries—screws holding toe bones together, plates stabilizing my ankles, feet, and an artificial heel in my left foot. Despite these setbacks, I maintained a positive outlook and my divine faith, which provided me with spiritual strength and resilience.

Four months after the accident, based on my determination, focus on the future, and the power of meditation supported by my faith in Gurus and Sai Baba Ji, I requested to transition to crutches. My request shocked my surgeon, who initially told me I wouldn't be able to walk. With my persistence, he agreed, and I transitioned from a wheelchair to crutches.

This progress demonstrated the importance of mental strength in physical recovery. I even managed to travel for work meetings across the country from the senior's home using crutches and air braces, showcasing my determination to regain normalcy. Inspired by my friend Richard's vision, who would always say, "Awtar, I saw you walking," and guided by an internal voice, I progressed to using canes five months later, continually surprising my medical team with my determination.

Interactions With Senior Residents

At the senior's home, I met numerous senior residents, mostly retired armed forces personnel from diverse backgrounds and professions. They had lived rich lives and shared fascinating stories—from owning businesses across continents to recounting their armed forces experiences. Despite their age and daily health challenges, these seniors were still full of life and always managed to smile. They called me "young lad" and consistently encouraged me.

I learned to tolerate pain without showing it, which in turn inspired these seniors. My positive attitude and resilience often put their own complaints into perspective, teaching them the power of maintaining hope and a positive outlook in the face of adversity. This mutual exchange of support and inspiration became an integral part of my recovery journey, highlighting the importance of community and shared experiences in the healing process.

As I became more adept at navigating the dining room in my wheelchair, which required careful maneuvering, the seniors would cheer me on, celebrating my successes.

These interactions not only boosted my morale but also fostered a sense of camaraderie and mutual support among the residents. The encouragement from my fellow residents created a positive environment conducive to healing and personal growth, reminding me that recovery is not just a physical process but also a communal journey of shared strength and resilience.

Going Home: A New Chapter in Recovery

After 12 months of intensive rehabilitation at the senior's home, my medical team and insurance company agreed that I was ready to continue my recovery at home while resuming work. This transition marked a significant milestone in my journey, reflecting the progress I had made both physically and mentally.

Throughout my stay at the senior's home, I cultivated a mindset of acceptance and resilience. Rather than dwelling on the circumstances of the accident, I chose to view my experience as part of a larger plan of the universe. This perspective, nurtured by my meditation practice and spiritual encounters, proved invaluable in navigating the complexities of my recovery.

As I prepared to leave the senior's home, my care was transferred from Dr. O'Neil to Dr. Brunei, a specialist in micro bone surgeries. This change in medical oversight signaled a new phase in my treatment, focusing on more intricate procedures to address the lingering effects of my injuries. Dr. Brunei's expertise in minimally invasive techniques, similar to those used in microdiscectomies and spinal fusions, offered hope for further improvements in my condition.

The transition home brought both excitement and new challenges. While I had made significant strides in my recovery, including progressing from a wheelchair to crutches and then to canes, I still faced ongoing medical needs. The prospect of balancing work responsibilities with continued rehabilitation and potential future surgeries loomed ahead. However, the strength I had gained from my experiences at the senior's home, coupled with the unwavering support of my family and colleagues, gave me the confidence to face these new challenges.

My journey, from the critical moments following the accident through my time at the senior's home, had been a testament to the power of holistic healing. The combination of traditional medical care, spiritual practices, and the support network I had built among the senior residents and staff had brought me to this point. As I prepared for the next chapter of my recovery, I carried with me not only the physical progress I had made but also the mental fortitude and spiritual growth I had cultivated during my time at the senior's home.

As I left the senior's home, I was not just returning to my previous life but stepping into a new phase of existence, armed with newfound strength and a deeper appreciation for life's challenges and blessings.

This transition marked not just a physical relocation but a symbolic step towards reclaiming my independence and reintegrating into my professional and personal life. The lessons learned and relationships formed during my time at the senior's home would continue to influence my approach to recovery and life in general, serving as a constant reminder of the power of perseverance and the importance of maintaining a positive outlook, even in the face of daunting circumstances.

Healing Journey: Physical Recovery and Emotional Resilience

The senior's home served as both a physical refuge for healing and a spiritual sanctuary where I could cultivate resilience through connection with divine guidance. This dual focus on physical recovery and spiritual awakening laid the groundwork for an extraordinary journey toward reclaiming my life against all odds.

Throughout this journey, support from friends and family played a vital role in my healing process. My friend Richard often told me, "He saw me walking in his dreams." This constant encouragement fueled my determination to recover and reinforced my belief in the power of positive thinking.

Embracing Meditation: A Pathway To Healing

During my time at the senior's home, I embraced meditation as a daily practice, introduced by our family friend Srinivasan Ji. The "So Hum" meditation technique became particularly beneficial, providing me with peace and tranquility amid physical pain and emotional turmoil. My daily practice involved dedicating 10 to 20 minutes to synchronize my breath with "SO" (inhale) and "Hum" (exhale) while focusing on visualizing my breath moving along the spine. The goal was to achieve union with the universal cosmic consciousness.

This practice helped increase calmness, clarity, and focus while decreasing anxiety and stabilizing emotions. Meditation contributed significantly to my recovery process, improving my concentration, attention to detail, and focus—skills that were crucial as I worked towards regaining my independence and ensuring my performance at work.

During one meditation session, I had an **extraordinary experience** that transcended the physical realm. This profound encounter included a vision of various spiritual figures and culminated in a meeting with a saint who offered reassurance and blessings. This event marked a turning point in my recovery journey, instilling a deep sense of hope and purpose. For a detailed account of this spiritual experience and its impact on my recovery, please refer to the meditation chapter.

Holistic Approach to Healing

The combination of meditation, my faith, and unwavering support created a robust foundation for my resilience during recovery. This holistic approach to healing— encompassing physical therapy, meditation, and emotional support—proved instrumental in reclaiming my life. It demonstrated that recovery is not just about physical healing but also about nurturing the mind and spirit.

> Recovery is not just about physical healing, but also about nurturing the mind and spirit.

My experience exemplifies the power of combining traditional medical care with holistic approaches. It illustrates how building resilience in recovery involves physical healing, emotional growth, and spiritual development. By prioritizing self-care, developing coping strategies, and maintaining a positive mindset, I navigated the challenges of recovery and legal battles, emerging stronger.

As I progressed in my recovery, transitioning from a wheelchair to crutches and eventually to canes—the spiritual insights gained through meditation and blessings from my divine powers continued to motivate and comfort me. The senior's home was not just a place of physical convalescence but a crucible for holistic healing—body, mind, and spirit. It was here that I learned to harness the power of meditation and spiritual connection, tools that would prove invaluable in the challenges that lay ahead. By integrating these elements into my life, I faced challenges with renewed purpose and optimism, leading to a more comprehensive and fulfilling healing process.

Chapter 6: A Global Embrace: The Power of Support in Recovery

During my time at the hospital and subsequent stay at the senior's home, I experienced an extraordinary outpouring of support that transcended borders and time. This global embrace played a crucial role in my recovery, offering comfort, motivation, and a profound sense of connection that helped me navigate the challenges of my rehabilitation.

Family and Professional Support

My immediate family formed the core of this support network. My mother stayed for months, providing unwavering care and emotional strength. My siblings, nieces, and nephews from both Canada and India offered their support, reminding me of the love and bonds that sustained me through difficult times.

The support extended into my professional life as well. Colleagues from Environment Canada visited regularly, bringing a sense of normalcy and connection to my work life. Remarkably, former colleagues from Nav Canada, where I had worked 20 years prior, made an unexpected visit with thoughtful gift baskets, demonstrating the enduring nature of professional relationships.

Global Outreach

As news of my accident spread, I received an outpouring of support from around the globe. Best wishes poured in from Russia, Germany, Denmark, the USA, India, and across Canada. Colleagues from various Ice Centers and Coast Guard offices globally reached out with messages of support. The wall of my room became a vibrant tapestry of cards and well-wishes while the table overflowed with flowers.

This global show of support not only lifted my spirits but also played an unexpected role in my legal journey. The impressive display of cards moved my lawyer, initially hesitant, to take on my case to defend me against charges of dangerous driving causing death.

Spiritual Support

The spiritual aspect of this support was particularly uplifting. Mr. Sandhu, a friend of my brother, would call weekly to read and explain Shabad (scriptures) from Guru Granth Sahib, bringing immense peace during challenging times. Other family friends sent pocket-sized versions of holy books, further nurturing my spiritual journey.

Srinivasan Ji, another family friend, offered support by focusing on spirituality and meditation. He reached out to his Guru in India to seek guidance for my recovery and consistently offered encouraging words, motivational thoughts, and insights on God and meditation. '

Impact and Reflection

This global embrace of support was truly transformative, helping me momentarily forget the gravity of my situation. The outpouring of love and support from around the world became a crucial element in my healing process, demonstrating the profound impact of human connection and compassion in the face of adversity.

Reflecting on this period, I am filled with immense gratitude. The support I received was not just comfort but a powerful force in my recovery journey. It reinforced my determination to heal and return to the communities - both personal and professional - that had shown such extraordinary care and concern. This global embrace became a testament to the strength found in human connections and the unexpected ways in which blessings can manifest during our darkest hours.

While my support came from a diverse global network rather than a formal mutual help organization, it demonstrates the power of community in the recovery process. The combination of family, professional, and spiritual support created a comprehensive network that addressed various aspects of my well-being.

Chapter 7: A Journey Through Meditation and Transformative Experience

As mentioned in the previous chapter on "Embracing Meditation," Srinivasan, a relative of family, introduced me to 'So Hum' Meditation, which became a transformative element in my recovery journey. Initially challenging due to my physical condition, this practice gradually evolved into a powerful tool for healing and self-discovery.

Overcoming Challenges Through Breath and Mantra

The 'So Hum' meditation technique synchronizes breath with mantra, calming the mind and improving concentration. Despite initial struggles with focus due to constant pain, I persevered. With each session, I delved deeper into practice and experienced a profound shift in my perception of physical limitations.

Focusing on the breath and mantra strengthened my mind-body connection, enhancing my awareness of my physical self. This heightened body awareness not only aided in my healing process but also supported my ability to engage effectively in rehabilitation and maintain a positive outlook.

The meditation practice I adopted during my time at the senior's home continued to be a source of strength long after my initial recovery. It bolstered my belief, faith, and willpower, allowing me to visualize better outcomes despite ongoing challenges. This spiritual practice, combined with support from Shabad (holy scriptures) readings and holy books, formed a robust foundation for my mental and emotional resilience.

My friend Richard's weekly visits and his recurring statement, "Awtar, I saw you walking yesterday in my dreams," served as a powerful positive affirmation. This external support complemented the internal strength I cultivated through meditation, creating a synergy that propelled my recovery forward.

In retrospect, integrating 'So Hum' meditation into my recovery journey exemplifies the power of holistic healing approaches. By combining traditional medical care with spiritual practices and unwavering support from loved ones, I was able to navigate the complex path of rehabilitation with greater resilience and hope.

The Extraordinary Vision

As my meditation practice advanced, I achieved a state where I could perceive an inner light traversing my chakras. This luminous energy would start from my lower chakra and ascend through my forehead chakra and crown, guiding me into a metaphysical tunnel. Within this passage, I was blessed with visions of Sai Baba Ji, many Gurus, spiritual guides, and other revered sages. This tunnel served as a conduit to the divine, offering uplifting encounters with God's messengers and instilling me with profound spiritual elevation. My journey would then transcend the tunnel, propelling me into the boundless expanse of the universe. In this state of cosmic consciousness, I found myself soaring over mountains, oceans, and lakes while exploring realms beyond earthly recognition. These transcendent experiences provided solace during my physical recovery and deepened my spiritual awakening, reinforcing my faith in the divine presence and the blessings that guided my path through this challenging period.

Sai Baba Ji Appears

Then came the moment that would solidify this transformation even further. One day, after finishing my 'So-Hum' meditation, I entered my usual semi-conscious state, which typically lasted about 20 minutes. During this subconscious state, I encountered a saint with an open hand bearing the sacred symbol, **"OM"**, whose presence radiated warmth and understanding. When he spoke, it wasn't with words but with a profound message that penetrated every cell of my being: *"Everything will be okay."* This encounter was not just a vision; it was a promise that resonated deeply within me, providing reassurance during moments of doubt and fear as I navigated the complexities of recovery and uncertainties. This Saint's blessings opened my consciousness while enhancing my cognition and compassion.

Curiosity and Confirmation

"Everything will be okay."

Filled with curiosity and anticipation, I turned to my laptop to search for information about this Saint. To my astonishment, the face I saw during my meditation matched the images of Sai Baba Ji, who appeared in my search results after many days of effort. This confirmation filled me with indescribable joy, validating the profound spiritual experience I had undergone.

Driven by this revelation, I delved deeper into

researching this divine power, downloading special prayers, and immersing myself in the teachings of Sai Baba Ji. This discovery marked a significant turning point in my life, igniting a passionate pursuit of spiritual knowledge and practice.

With growing excitement, I shared my extraordinary experience with friends and family, proudly recounting the miraculous encounter. As days passed, my faith in Sai Baba Ji and the power of meditation grew stronger, fueling an unwavering determination to accelerate my recovery. This spiritual awakening not only provided comfort during my physical rehabilitation but also instilled in me a profound sense of purpose and connection to the divine, transforming my approach to life's challenges and deepening my understanding of the interconnectedness of mind, body, and spirit.

Looking back on this period at the senior's home, I realize that meditation did more than help me cope with physical pain; it opened doors to understanding myself and the interconnectedness of physical, mental, and spiritual well-being. The 'So Hum' meditation, combined with profound spiritual experiences, became cornerstones of my healing journey, aligning seamlessly with the transformative practice discussed earlier.

Reflections On Transformation

This chapter of meditation and spiritual awakening laid the groundwork for an extraordinary journey toward reclaiming my life against all odds. It exemplifies how combining traditional medical care with holistic approaches like meditation can facilitate profound healing—physically, emotionally, and spiritually.

Sai Baba's message, ***"Everything will be okay,"*** resonated deeply, reinforcing the positive outlook I had cultivated through meditation. With this assurance, I never looked back, moving forward as if nothing had happened—defying all odds. My friends and coworkers were frequently astonished to see me engaging in regular duties at work and home despite my injuries. Remarkably, I traveled the world using canes and air casts while maintaining an active social life.

Meditation transformed not only my approach to recovery but also how I viewed life itself—***full of potential and unlimited possibilities.*** My journey became an example for those around me; they found courage in witnessing my determination to face challenges head-on despite the obstacles. This created a ripple effect of hope and resilience, inspiring others to face their own hurdles.

Through this transformative experience in meditation, I discovered that faith is not merely a belief but an active force that shapes our reality. The blessings I received instilled in me unwavering willpower that became evident in every aspect of my life—a testament to how embracing spirituality can illuminate even the darkest paths we walk on our journeys toward healing and self-discovery.

This profound realization aligns with the holistic healing approach I had adopted, combining traditional medical care with spiritual practices and the unwavering support of friends and family.

Chapter 8: Mistaken Identity: A Perilous Journey in India

As I lay in my bed at the senior's home, recovering from a recent hospital visit for wound cleaning and plaster changes, exhaustion overwhelmed me. The specialized transport had just brought me back on a stretcher, as I was still prohibited from bearing weight on my feet. As fatigue took over, I drifted into sleep, and vivid memories from my 1989 trip to India began to flood my consciousness.

The Airport Ordeal

The flashback transported me to Delhi's Indira Gandhi International Airport. It was August 1989, five years after Operation Blue Star and the assassination of Prime Minister Indira Gandhi, events that had intensified the Khalistan movement. I was traveling from Canada with my two sons, Ranjeet (14) and Pardeep (10), while my wife Praveena had preceded us to India by a week.

Upon our morning arrival at the airport, I approached the immigration counter. The officer stamped my passport but then abruptly confiscated it, instructing me to wait. After all the other passengers from our flight had cleared, immigration officers began interrogating me. *"Do you know these individuals involved in the hijacking of an Indian Airlines flight to Lahore?"* they demanded, mentioning specific names.

Shocked and terrified, I vehemently denied any knowledge, condemning such acts of cowardice. My frightened children began to cry as they worried about me. This ordeal stretched for three hours before my courageous wife managed to reach the immigration area, requesting our children's release while I remained in custody.

The situation deteriorated when the next shift commander, after six hours in detention, moved me to a dimly lit room without any windows. A misunderstanding arose when the same officer inquired if I had any "biscuits," and I said 'No,' as I assumed he was talking about cookies. Later, I realized "biscuits" were code for gold bars. The subsequent three hours were terrifying.

The Rescue Efforts

Meanwhile, my wife contacted friends in Canada, setting in motion a chain of interventions. One friend reached out to a businessman in Delhi, who contacted senior immigration officials in India; another sent a telex from Canada to the Canadian High Commissioner in India, and a third roused the Indian High Commissioner in Ottawa from sleep, who got in touch with Indian foreign affairs.

After more than ten grueling hours, Interpol personnel arrived, ordering me to take the luggage to the second floor, a windowless room. They meticulously examined my luggage, photographed and fingerprinted me, and scrutinized my address book. They were looking for contacts related to the Air India hijack incident in my address book but got disappointed when they didn't find any. Upon discovering no incriminating evidence, they finally released me. The young Interpol senior officer impressed me, assuring me that I was now clear and there wouldn't be any questions in the future. He also helped me clear the immigration check-out. *Later, I would find out this was all a lie.*

Journey To Ludhiana

We spent that night in Delhi, and I got in touch with my brother in Ludhiana, explaining the events that had unfolded at the airport and the accusations against me. He advised us against going to our village, where my parents were waiting, suspecting that the police might be looking for me there.

The next day, all four of us, along with my sister-in-law (my brother's wife from Calgary), who accompanied us from Delhi, journeyed to Ludhiana via train to stay with my brother. Upon reaching the Guru Nanak Engineering College campus, we faced another *frightening encounter*. The campus gates were locked, and as I exited our car to ask the gatekeeper to open the gate, I suddenly found myself staring down the barrels of Punjab Police guns. My wife and sister-in-law, frightened, shouted for me to get back in the car. After explaining the purpose of our visit, they allowed us to enter the campus but warned us that Indian Central Police Forces were stationed inside with *shoot-on-sight* orders.. We later learned that a police officer had been killed on campus, heightening tensions.

As we drove towards my brother's unit, masked, armed central police halted us again and questioned the purpose of our trip and destination. We provided satisfactory answers. They initially demanded that we walk to my brother's residence, which was only a few hundred feet away, carrying our luggage. When we requested their help, they relented and let us drive.

The Aftermath

The next day, I ventured out to find the campus resembling a war zone, with police stations scattered throughout—a chilling reminder of the volatile situation in Punjab. These experiences cast a long shadow over what should have been a joyous family reunion, altering our perception of home and safety. While in Ludhiana, my parents came to see us there. They explained that our decision not to come to the village was wise and had saved us. They further revealed that the police had been looking for me in the village. They thanked God that we were safe.

> Punjab police were looking for me in our village

Throughout this trip, I developed a fear of the unknown. When returning to Canada, the Indian immigration officer again detained me and questioned me for at least 30 minutes before giving clearance to proceed. I was really scared and felt a sigh of relief when the plane left Indian air space.

I traveled to India again in 1998 and frequently from 2003 onwards. Until 2010, I was always stopped at the immigration counter and questioned, as they were still looking for Awtar Singh. *Later, I discovered the real person had left India many years ago and he was still active in those incriminating activities in Canada.*

In the 2010s, India modernized its manual entry systems to state-of-the-art advanced systems capable of thorough identity verification. Thanks to this, I was never questioned again, as my innocence was finally recognized by technology.

As I slowly woke from this vivid flashback, I found myself back in my familiar surroundings—on my bed in the senior home, with both feet hanging in the air, and in plasters. Despite the lingering fear of reliving those memories, I felt a sense of relief to be back in the present, safe from the turmoil of the past. As a result of this fear, the pain in my feet had exponentially increased, requiring another painkiller to get this crucial pain under control. In this moment of distress, my faith, the universe's blessings, and my Guru's blessings helped me return to a normal state, providing comfort and reassurance in the face of these haunting memories.

Chapter 9: The Legal Labyrinth – a test of Resilence

During my year-long stay at the hospital and senior's residence, I faced a series of challenging developments that compounded the stress of my recovery. The gravity of the situation became apparent when a detective and police officer visited me in the hospital to take my statement regarding the accident. Their skepticism was palpable as I recounted the events truthfully, and it was then that I officially learned of the grave charges against me – "dangerous driving causing death."

Recognizing the seriousness of the situation, my father-in-law wisely advised my wife to retain a good lawyer while I was still in the hospital. She secured competent legal representation by McLelland, but he said that his decision to take my case would be based on visiting me in the convalescent facility, i.e., the senior home.

The legal implications quickly escalated. My wife brought me legal papers in the senior home from the deceased driver's family lawyer, seeking $1.5 million in damages, an astronomical amount at that time. This civil suit added another layer of complexity to the ongoing criminal case in Renfrew County. The criminal charges against me were all over the news, intensifying public scrutiny and adding to our stress.

Legal Representation and Strategy

One day, our lawyer, McLelland, came to see me and my wife in the senior home to decide if he was willing to take on my serious criminal charges case. His approach was particularly touching. After interviewing us, he agreed to represent me. What really convinced him to take our case was the sight of the white walls covered with cards from around the globe and the presence of friends visiting me. We were incredibly fortunate that he accepted our case, given its complexity and potential challenges.

McLelland provided crucial insight, suggesting that the charges might be influenced by racial bias. He pointed out that "a brown man driving a Cadillac through Renfrew County" might not be well-received in that area. This perspective highlighted the potential challenges we faced in seeking a fair trial in the lower court in Renfrew County and added an unsettling layer of complexity to an already challenging situation.

Court Appearances and Legal Strategy

My first court appearance in Renfrew County, about three months after the accident, was grueling. I was on crutches, with plasters on both feet, and in intense pain. My wife, father-in-law, and friend Richard accompanied me, providing much-needed support. McLelland's astute legal strategy became clear during the second appearance. Recognizing the potential for bias, discrimination, and possible favoritism, as the deceased was from Renfrew County, he advised me to request a transfer to the Superior Court of Ontario in Pembroke. When the judge asked if I would like to continue the case in her court, I followed my lawyer's advice and requested a transfer to the superior court, which she granted.

After the case was transferred to the Superior Court, monthly appearances in Pembroke, approximately 100 km away from Kanata, became routine. These brief, 15-minute sessions often resulted in new court dates, prolonging the process. On occasions when my lawyer failed to appear in court, I experienced dread, unaware that this was part of his strategy to buy time and build our case.

There were numerous painful court appearances throughout this period. At one point, there was a possibility that my son, who was with me during the accident, might be called a witness. However, thanks to my lawyer's experience - or perhaps divine intervention - he was exempted from testifying, as he didn't see much beyond us following the truck. I later learned that the truck driver, who was the main witness, had not stayed at the accident site but had left the scene. He reportedly messaged all drivers in his gas delivery fleet to avoid that part of Highway 17 near Renfrew, a fact that would later prove significant in our case.

Throughout this challenging time, I maintained my practice of 'So Hum' meditation, which proved transformative, offering profound insights and connections to my past. The support of my family, friends, and colleagues provided a crucial lifeline, reminding me that I wasn't facing these trials alone.

Unable to drive due to the condition of my feet, I relied on air braces and crutches. My lawyer would regularly drive me to Pembroke to discuss my case, impressing me with his thoughtfulness and attention to detail.

In August 2002, court attendance became particularly challenging and painful following my second surgery. This period of my life, while incredibly difficult, demonstrated the importance of resilience, faith, willpower, support systems, and strategic thinking in navigating complex legal and personal situations. It also highlighted how meditation and spiritual practices can provide strength and insight during trying times, even as the legal troubles continued to brew beneath the surface of my outwardly supportive network. The experience would forever change my perspective on life, justice, and the power of perseverance.

Final Decision: A Turning Point in the Legal Labyrinth

In late 2002, the culmination of our legal journey arrived. My lawyer drove to Pembroke, instructing us to travel separately. My wife, friend Richard, and I joined him, our nerves on edge despite the faith that had sustained me throughout this ordeal.

As our turn approached in the courtroom, my lawyer employed a permissible strategy under character evidence rules. He asked the judge to allow me to testify about my character, experience, values, and work at Environment Canada. This approach allows for defendants in criminal cases to negate a charge of criminal conduct. My testimony seemed to satisfy the judge, setting a positive tone for the proceedings.

The cross-examination of the truck driver, the sole witness, revealed a crucial weakness in the prosecution's case. He contradicted his previous statement, initially claiming my car was beside him when he was driving in the right lane but now expressing uncertainty and suggesting I was further back. This inconsistency significantly undermined the witness's credibility.

A pivotal moment came during the police officer's presentation of the accident scene. While the officer emphasized that at the time of the accident, I was driving on Highway 17, a two-lane highway typically marked with double solid lines prohibiting passing, he incorrectly assumed I was attempting to pass the truck.

My astute lawyer scrutinized the images of the highway where the accident happened and pointed out a critical detail - there were no lines visible where the accident occurred, which implied no clear restrictions on lane changes at that specific location. This revelation cast significant doubt on the prosecution's narrative.

My lawyer assertively argued that it was the truck driver who should face charges for causing the accident.

After weighing up the evidence and arguments presented, the judge announced he would reconvene in three weeks to deliver his verdict.

When we returned to Ontario Superior Court in Pembroke to hear the verdict, the judge meticulously explained the factors considered in his decision. He carefully reviewed his findings, addressing each element of the charges against me. After this thorough analysis, to our immense relief, he declared, *"Not guilty."*

Concerned about our safety due to the other party's visible anger at the verdict, our lawyer advised us to wait in the courtroom for 30 minutes before escorting us to our car. This final act of protection underscored the gravity of the situation we had navigated.

This experience reinforced the power of perseverance and skilled legal representation in the face of seemingly insurmountable odds. It stands as a testament to the importance of thorough investigation and the unpredictable nature of legal proceedings, where a single detail can alter the course of justice.

Chapter 10: Employer Support and Balancing Act at Environment Canada

As news of my accident spread, it sent shockwaves through my workplace at the Canadian Ice Service (CIS), a division of the Meteorological Service of Canada (MSC) within Environment and Climate Change Canada. My colleagues and management quickly informed the MSC offices about the severity of my condition, initially anticipating that I might not return to work. My director even began preparing disability paperwork for Sunlife, the government insurance company, expecting a prolonged recovery period.

Unwavering Support from Colleagues

During my hospital stay and subsequent transfer to the senior's home, I experienced unwavering support from my colleagues. They visited regularly, sharing best wishes from across the MSC. As my condition improved, these visits evolved into weekly Friday gatherings where we discussed work and office happenings—a significant morale booster that I deeply appreciated. This sense of community and human connection played a vital role in my recovery.

Returning to Work: A Crucial Step

Two months after the accident, I insisted on resuming my professional duties as a manager of the IT section of the CIS. I viewed returning to work as a crucial step in my overall rehabilitation. My employer was supportive of a gradual transition, understanding the seriousness of my recovery process. However, my insurance company initially resisted, fearing potential setbacks. I eventually convinced them by demonstrating that returning to work would reduce their costs—an approach they seemed unaccustomed to.

My return to work showcased my employer's exceptional support. They modified all entrances, my office, and washrooms to accommodate my wheelchair needs, allowing me to maneuver comfortably. The transition wasn't easy; fatigue and pain medication side effects were challenging. However, my colleagues and management remained extremely supportive and cooperative. Despite my director having completed disability papers, I refused to go on disability, believing it would have been detrimental to my recovery and mental well-being.

Navigating Challenges

My work ethic, shaped by my private industry background, was results-oriented, which sometimes clashed with the public sector culture. The complex technologies used in our workplace required specialized skills that some struggled with or were missing entirely. To address this gap, I relied on external private sector expertise to help deliver solutions that met business needs.

Despite these challenges and ongoing legal pressures, returning to work proved to be a positive change. Team-building lunches and daily interactions with colleagues provided a sense of normalcy. Immersing myself in work that I loved offered satisfaction and a mental escape from both legal troubles and physical fatigue.

Professional Growth and Opportunities

Within two years, my legal matters had concluded, and I was traveling nationally and internationally using air casts and canes for meetings and conferences. I presented papers at conferences on real-time systems showcasing the CIS's implementation of state-of-the-art decision support systems. These opportunities were a testament to my employer's support and trust in my abilities.

Subsequently, I was assigned as a senior project manager for another project in the Director-General's office, where I enjoyed bringing in outstanding resources from the CIS to help deliver the initial stages of this project. My assignments continued to provide similar opportunities for participation in national and international projects. Although I was still recovering and facing permanent mobility issues, these professional engagements were instrumental in maintaining both my skills and cognitive sharpness.

Gratitude for Support and Encouragement

Working with the management, operations, and IT teams at the CIS was a joy despite occasional obstacles. Their unwavering support played a crucial role in my recovery and professional growth. The collaborative environment fostered by my colleagues made it easier for me to navigate challenges while reinforcing our shared commitment to delivering effective solutions that met real-time operational demands.

I would like to express my heartfelt gratitude to the management, IT teams, operations staff at the Canadian Ice Service, and the Director-General of the Meteorological Service of Canada. Their encouragement and trust were vital during this challenging period of my recovery and for regaining confidence as well as continuing professional development.

Chapter 11: Conclusion: A Journey of Joy, Resilience, and Transformation

From 2005 to 2019, life unfolded in a beautifully normal rhythm filled with joy, meaningful milestones, and family growth. Despite ongoing health challenges, including multiple surgeries and the sobering news in 2007 that further operations were no longer possible, I refused to let my physical condition define me.

During this time frame, my wife and I traveled to India six times for various reasons, including business development and preparations for our son's wedding. The celebration of my elder son's marriage in 2005 brought our family together in happiness. In 2007, the arrival of twins added even more joy to our lives. We witnessed both of our sons graduating and settling into their respective paths, with our eldest thriving in the Canadian Navy—a source of immense pride for us.

Throughout the years, my wife and I embraced opportunities to travel the world, taking cruises that allowed us to explore new cultures and create lasting memories together. Our beloved dog, Bruiser, was a cherished companion during these adventures. He brought joy and warmth to our journeys until he left us at the age of seventeen.

However, life took an unexpected turn in September 2019 when my elder son fell seriously ill. His journey through stage 4 pancreatic cancer, compounded by a devastating house fire and the isolation of the COVID-19 pandemic, tested our family's resilience profoundly. His passing in July 2020 left an indelible mark on our lives.

Since then, I've experienced vivid visions and dreams where he communicated with me in ways that felt incredibly real, providing comfort and connection during an incredibly difficult time.

Reflecting on this journey, I've come to believe that our experiences—both challenging and joyful—serve a greater purpose within the universe's grand design. Each of us has a unique mission in life that the universe has set before us. While we may not always understand the reasons behind our trials, I've learned to accept these as opportunities for growth and transformation.

My experiences have taught me that every challenge is a chance to become stronger, wiser, and more compassionate. Through recovery and personal losses, I've discovered reservoirs of strength I never knew I possessed. These experiences have shaped me as an individual and deepened my understanding of the universe's interconnectedness.

I now see life as a continuous journey of learning and growth. Each obstacle overcome has brought me closer to understanding my purpose within the cosmic tapestry. The joy of family milestones, alongside the heartbreak of loss, has been integral to this journey, driving me to persevere in adversity while cherishing moments of joy.

Above all, these experiences have solidified my belief in the universe's guiding force. This faith has provided comfort during difficult times and gratitude during moments of triumph. It reminds me daily that we are part of something greater than ourselves and that our lives have meaning beyond what we can see or understand.

This perspective has not only helped me navigate my own challenges but has also inspired me to assist others in finding their strength and purpose within the universe's design. Through my interactions with others, I strive to share the lessons I've learned about resilience and faith in a higher purpose.

The vivid dreams and visions of my son after his passing have further reinforced my belief in the interconnectedness of all things and the continuity of spirit within the universe. These experiences have added a new dimension to my understanding of life, death, and the enduring power of love.

This journey has taught me to embrace each day as an opportunity to grow, contribute, and love— regardless of the challenges that may arise. In doing so, I believe we align ourselves with the universe's grand design, playing our unique part in the cosmic symphony of existence.

"When Hope Fades: A Son's Journey Through Pain and Loss."

"From Earthly Struggles to Eternal Connections"

I look forward to sharing my son's journey in my upcoming book: "*When Hope Fades: A Son's Journey Through Pain and Loss - From Earthly Struggles to Eternal Connections.*" This story explores how our earthly trials can lead to profound spiritual growth and a deeper understanding of our place in the universe.

The book will delve into the significant challenges my son faced: the life-altering fire, his diagnosis with stage 4 pancreatic cancer, the grueling treatments he endured, and the emotional toll of battling cancer during a global pandemic. Through these trials, we discovered that suffering can be a catalyst for transformation, softening our rough edges and helping us value what truly matters in life.

As a father, I witnessed how these earthly struggles forged an unbreakable bond between us and ultimately led to a spiritual awakening. In our darkest moments, we found an inexplicable peace and hope that transcended physical limitations. This journey taught us that while suffering can shake our faith, it also has the power to strengthen it, producing endurance, character, and hope.

Our story illustrates how, in the face of immense pain and loss, we can find connection not only with each other but also with the Creator. It's a testament to the idea that our earthly challenges can open pathways to eternal truths and a deeper spiritual connection. Through this book, I aim to share how our experience of love and connection extended beyond the boundaries of this life, offering a message of hope and resilience to others facing similar struggles.

In the wake of my son's untimely passing, I have experienced profound visions and dreams that have allowed me to maintain a connection with him beyond this physical realm. These experiences have deepened my understanding of the soul's immortality and the universal interconnectedness that binds us all. I believe that while we are living, part of our soul remains with us, while another part is woven into the fabric of the universe.

Ultimately, this journey has taught me to embrace each day as an opportunity for growth, connection, and love—regardless of the challenges that may arise. In doing so, I believe we align ourselves with the universe's grand design, playing our unique part in its cosmic symphony

About the Author

Born in Punjab, India, Awtar Singh Koonar earned his degree in Electrical Engineering before relocating to Canada in 1971. He furthered his education with a master's degree in electrical engineering and computer science. Koonar began his professional career as a software engineer for the Canadian Air Traffic Control System, where he gained invaluable experience in critical systems.

He later joined Environment Canada, where he held various positions, including System Analyst, System Manager, Software Development Manager, Project Manager, and Head of the IT Branch. His career culminated as a Senior Projects Portfolio Manager, overseeing significant initiatives that enhanced national capabilities.

After retiring, Koonar embraced his entrepreneurial spirit, engaging in training and the development of adaptive decision support frameworks. He also served as a Senior Project Manager Consultant for various organizations, leveraging his expertise to drive successful project outcomes.

Throughout his career, Koonar has provided consulting services in project management in North America. He co-developed ITIL educational curricula for a major education provider and has taught ITIL and project management courses throughout North America. He is a licensed professional engineer with the Association of Professional Engineers of Ontario and holds several certifications: Project Management Professional (PMP), Certified Scrum Master (CSM), ITIL Expert, ITIL Managing Professional (MP), and Scaled Agile Framework (SAFe 5). His expertise has enabled him to manage multiple businesses offering project management, geospatial, and IT service management (ITSM) services.

He has published numerous papers in scientific, IT, geospatial, and networking journals. Inspired by friends and his own experiences, Koonar authored his first book, "Unbreakable Spirit: From Shadows to Radiance,"

Upcoming Publications

1. "When Hope Fades: A Son's Journey Through Pain and Loss: From Earthly Struggles to Eternal Connections" by Awtar Singh Koonar (forthcoming)

2. "Adaptive Decision Intelligence: Unlocking Value through Digital Transformation and Decision Enablers" by Awtar Singh Koonar (forthcoming)

3. "Value Delivery Through Adaptive Decision Intelligence: Leveraging Enablers and Decision Support Framework for Digital Transformation" by Awtar Singh Koonar (forthcoming)